HONORÉE CORDER

I MUST WRITE MY BOOK

THE COMPANION WORKBOOK TO
YOU MUST WRITE A BOOK

ALSO BY HONORÉE CORDER

Like a Boss book series

Write Like a Boss: From a Whisper to a Roar

Publish Like a Boss: From Mind to Market

Market Like a Boss: From Book to Blockbuster

—

You Must Write a Book:
Boost Your Brand, Get More Business, and Become the Go-To Expert

The Prosperous Writer book series

Prosperity for Writers:
A Writer's Guide to Creating Abundance

Prosperity for Writer's Productivity Journal

The Nifty 15: Write Your Book in Just 15 Minutes a Day!

The Prosperous Writer's Guide to Making More Money:
Habits, Tactics, and Strategies for Making a Living as a Writer

The Prosperous Writer's Guide to Finding Readers:
Build Your Author Brand, Raise Your Profile and Find Readers to Delight

—

Business Dating: Applying Relationship Rules in Business
for Ultimate Success

Tall Order: Organize Your Life and Double Your Success
in Half the Time

Vision to Reality: How Short Term Massive Action Equals
Long Term Maximum Results

The Divorced Phoenix: Rising from the Ashes of a Broken Marriage

If Divorce is a Game, These are the Rules: 8 Rules for Thriving
Before, During and After Divorce

The Successful Single Mom book series

The Miracle Morning book series

HONORÉE CORDER

I
MUST
WRITE
MY BOOK

THE COMPANION WORKBOOK TO
YOU MUST WRITE A BOOK

Published by Honorée Enterprises Publishing

Cover design: Dino Marino ☙ Interior design: Dino Marino

Tradepaper ISBN: 978-0-9980731-3-2
Digital ISBN: 978-0-9980731-4-9

March 2019

TABLE OF CONTENTS

Special Invitation

I'd like to personally invite you to join the Prosperity for Writers Mastermind at HonoreeCorder.com/Writers and Facebook.com/groups/ProsperityforWriters where you will find motivation, daily support, and help with any writing or self-publishing questions.

You can connect with me personally on Twitter @Honoree, or on Facebook.com/Honoree. Thank you so much for your most precious resource, your time. I look forward to connecting and hearing about your book soon!

> **BE SURE TO SIGN UP FOR INSTANT ACCESS FOR ALL THE PUBLISHING RESOURCES I INCLUDE IN THIS BOOK!**
>
> Just visit: www.HonoreeCorder.com/youmustbonuses

How to Use This Workbook

Chances are you have read (or are reading) *You Must Write a Book* and are inspired to write your own book. Congratulations on making a decision that can change your life in unimaginable ways! The original book, and this workbook, are designed to help you almost as though I were walking you through the process one-on-one. (If you haven't yet read *You Must Write a Book*, you will need it as this is *not* a stand-alone workbook. You can get it by visiting HonoreeCorder.com/youmustwriteabook.)

The advanced readers of *You Must Write a Book* found themselves thinking *I need to write that down* and *I'll need a journal to remember this information and write my own book.* I was inspired to craft this workbook as an accompaniment to *You Must Write a Book* so you, too, can write, publish and launch your book as easily, effortlessly, and quickly as possible.

Every step you need to take is here in this Workbook. From concept to launch, from ebook to marketing, and everything in between, you'll find it in here!

In fact, you'll find all the necessary steps, as well as three timeline options.

I suggest you page all the way through this Workbook, and then start back at Chapter 1: First Things First, where you'll pick your track from three options:

- Holy Time-Warp Batman Track of 100 days
- Faster-than-Normal Track of 180 days
- Steady-As-You-Go Track of 365 days

I've included detailed timelines for each option, including due dates for each piece of the book publishing puzzle. All you must do, then, is work backwards from your target publishing date, and get to work.

Time a-wastin' – let's get *your* book started, shall we?

—Honorée
You Must Write a Book
www.HonoreeCorder.com

— 1 —

First Things First:

Before I Write My Book

There are several things to consider *before* you put pen to paper (or fingers to keyboard).

Before you write your book, you must ask yourself the following two questions:

1. What do you want the book to do for you? i.e., *What's in it for you?* In other words, do you want to sell the book and earn income *or* use the book to market your core business *or* both?

2. What action do you want the readers of your book to take? i.e., Do you want them to hire you? Buy another product or service you offer? Refer new business to you?

The answers to these two questions will inform and influence every other step you take in the process of creating your book.

Now, answer those two questions:

1. What Do You Want from Your Book?

What do you want the book to do for you? What do you want from your book? What specific goals do you have in life and business, and how will your book support those goals?

For example: *Provide an additional stream of income. Drive new business. Allow me to help more people. Give me better brand recognition. Bring in more clients or customers. Open doors to speaking engagements or high-fee consulting. Sell lots of books and make money from book sales. Make me the go-to expert in my field.*

Your book can replace your business card, become a stream or multiple streams of income, or all of the above.

What I want from my book is … (i.e., What I want from this book is an additional $1,000 or $10,000 a month in book sales income. Or, what I want from this book is $25,000 or $250,000 in new client revenue.)

_____

_____

_____

_____

_____

_____

_____

_____

_____

You can be as outrageous or realistic as you'd like, and if you need it, you have my permission to think BIG, dream BIGGER, and turn your vision to reality!

Remember this: Any goal you ink for your book has been actualized by someone else. There are many first-time authors who have quadrupled the size of their businesses, or sold tens of thousands of copies and earned a significant income from their books. It's up to you to decide what you truly want for and from your book, and own it!

Write down what you want from your book:

_____

_____

_____

_____

_____

_____

_____

_____

2. What action(s) do you want the readers of your book to take, not take, or both, as a result of reading your book?

In your book, you will either be solving a problem or problems, or giving advice, or both. Because of the problems you're solving, or the advice you're giving, you'll want your readers to take an action or actions (or avoid taking some!) based on the content of your book. Among the reasons you want to write a book, I would imagine you'll want people to engage you and/or purchase your products and/or services.

For example: For *You Must Write a Book*, I wanted every reader to write and professionally self-publish their own book. And I wanted them to avoid making some of the amateur mistakes I had made and still see others making.

Define your desired reader actions here:

The actions I want my readers to take are to: i.e., *Engage me to provide their corporate documents or financial plans.*

_____

_____

_____

_____

The actions I want my readers to *avoid taking* are:

_____

_____

_____

_____

Next, let's consider how much you can earn from your books.

CALCULATE POTENTIAL INCOME FROM SELLING BOOKS

If you're simply going to sell books, you'll make the retail price (minus costs) from any books you sell directly.

The general going price of an ebook is between 99 cents and $9.99. You can sell these on your website (and you'll provide them in these three formats: PDF, .epub (for Apple, Kobo, and other devices), and .mobi (for any Amazon Kindle device or app). Through these retail sites you'll earn 65% and 70% of the retail price respectively.

Your paperback's price can range from as low as $5.99 to $19.99 (and as you can see, $29.99 for a workbook). When you sell through Amazon, you'll earn 45% of the retail price.

The hard cost of your books (printing plus shipping) when using CreateSpace will be based upon the size of the book and number of pages. For example, on the low end, I've paid $2.19 for a single copy of a 6x9 book that is 220 pages, and $3.47 for an 8.5x11-sized workbook that is 108 pages. Selling both of those books at $19.99 provides a profit of $17.80 and $16.52 (before shipping costs). You can calculate how much you'll earn selling 10, 100, or 5000 copies.

CALCULATE YOUR PROJECTED INCOME FOR:

One book: _____

Book sales goal _____ x $ (profit) = _____ **projected**

income.

Calculate potential income from using books to generate new business:

_____

_____

_____

_____

_____

Separately, you can potentially earn significant income by using your book as a business generation tool.

Example: As an executive coach charging $1,000 per hour, I could give books away to 400 prospective clients or strategic partners, and still break even selling just one hour of coaching. Considering I was selling packages of eight sessions, and I would share an average of 50 books a month for a total cost of $125 (before shipping costs, which could include mailing the books at a cost of about $2.25 per book, which doubled the cost), my ROI was very high.

What is your projected new business revenue:

_____

_____

_____

_____

_____

Options for Writing the Book

You have multiple options when it comes to writing the book, here are three. Choose the one that works best for you. As a reminder, it is best for you to read *You Must Write a Book* in its entirety, so you understand the full process, even if you don't do much of the writing, publishing, or even launching yourself.

- **Write it yourself.** This option means while you are simultaneously crafting your book, you will also be working on the production, publication, and launch of the book as well.

- **Hire a ghostwriter or content creation specialist.** A great ghostwriter can work with you to identify your message, craft the tone and contents of the book, and produce a final fantastic product. And, then there are folks who specialize turning your expertise into a book you can hold in your hands, as well as create post-publication content to drive sales and help you get more clients. This type of investment ($20,000-$100,000 or more), is a custom option that can yield multiple dividends.

A Note About Writer's Block

I don't believe writer's block exists. As a financial advisor, lawyer, or mechanical engineer, you don't have financial, legal, or engineering block, right? However, it is reasonable that if this is your first time writing a book, you might experience the occasional lack of confidence or not have the certainty you need that you can, indeed, write your book.

I suggest if you have any hesitation or reservation about writing your book, you get your self-talk in order right away. I'm going to suggest two extremely effective action items you can take to make that happen:

1. Read the book *The Power of Consistency* by Weldon Long. Weldon's book will help you shut the door on any limiting beliefs you have (related or unrelated to book writing).
2. Read *The Miracle Morning for Writers* by Hal Elrod, Steve Scott (and me).

> The most successful people in the world *control* their mindset, *strengthen* their bodies, and *raise* their energy … intentionally and every single day. You need to do the same to achieve your potential *and write your book.*

To write your book during the time-frame you will shortly choose, and make a lasting impact on your success long-term, you must create a ritual that empowers you to take on every day at a Level 10. Your Level 10 means you are physically, mentally, and emotionally ready to take on anything – *anything* – that comes your way during the day. You might like it, love it, or hate it, but you are ready for it. To accomplish that, I suggest you incorporate *The Miracle Morning* into your day.

If you have ever faced a day with uncertainty and doubt, or not feeling at your absolute best, *you have missed untold and unquantified opportunities.* When I realized I was missing out on opportunities: to impact the lives of others, to accomplish all I wanted to do in this lifetime (including write lot of books), and as a by-product, relationships and revenues and experiences, I knew I had to take charge of my mind, body, and energy. Whether you will finish your book (or not) will be at least partially determined by whether (or not) you engage in a daily success ritual. The Miracle Morning ritual can and will become your daily habit of programming your mind, body, and energy levels for success. This programming means eventually you will perform at new levels <u>automatically</u>. When you combine the additional strategies specifically for writers in *The Miracle Morning for Writers* with what you'll learn in *The Power of Consistency*, you will be unstoppable--when it comes to writing your book, and in every other area of your life as well.

Once you have your mindset and beliefs handled, you'll be automatically inclined to take the actions necessary to write your book. And speaking of the actions you need to take to write your book, here they are:

SCHEDULE TIME TO WRITE EVERY DAY.

At this point, you can connect your everyday schedule to your goal of writing a book. Identify either:

- A time every day you schedule to write:_____

- A recurring time on your calendar every (circle one) **day week** to schedule the next day's or week's writing appointments.

SET A PUBLICATION GOAL DATE.

Intended publication date: _____

Note: This date may change! You will be well-served, however, to set a goal date even if you need to change it in the future.

To further assure you will follow through, be sure to take a moment and announce your intended publication date on Facebook or even LinkedIn. Garner some public support! Be sure to get the support of an accountability partner (preferably someone who is also writing a book) or a coach to help make sure you accomplish your goal on schedule.

SET A DAILY WORD COUNT GOAL.

Using 50,000 as your final word count goal (non-fiction books generally range between 40,000-50,000), and based on your timeframe (you'll dive into this more in Chapter 3), note your daily word count goal:

_____

Note: I give a complete overview of each Track in Chapter Three. This is just to give you an idea.

Based upon a target of finishing the first rough draft at the 60% mark (days 60, 108, and 219 of each time-frame listed in this book), here is your daily target word count:

- 100: 833
- 180: 463
- 365: 228

As you can see, the target word counts for your book, no matter which track you choose, are completely reasonable.

ONE MORE THING: CONSIDER THE CONSEQUENCES OF NOT WRITING YOUR BOOK

I can promise you won't regret writing your book, and I believe there is much more at stake for you if you don't. The goal here is to connect you with what happens *if you don't write your book*. What do you have to lose? Who, besides you, will lose out?

What are the consequences of not writing your book?

_____

_____

_____

_____

Who will miss out on the knowledge you possess that could truly benefit?

_____

_____

_____

_____

How many lives will you forgo helping if you don't make the time?

_____

_____

_____

Let me finish by saying you cannot possibly know what won't happen if you don't write your book, how many opportunities won't pop up, how many relationships you won't develop, or how many clients you won't be able to help. I urge you not to find out!

– 2 –

CRAFTING MY BOOK

After you've identified what you want from your book, and projected your book's income, it is time to begin crafting your book. Undoubtedly you will have multiple approaches to choose from, and a variety of topics you could include in your book. Let's drill down what will go in your *first* book. And, if you get the "bug" for writing more books, as many do, that's quite okay. It happens to the best of us!

The content of your book will be solely based upon your desired outcome(s) for the book. Nothing more, nothing less.

CRAFTING YOUR BOOK

ARE YOU:

Solving problems? If so, which ones:

_____

_____

_____

_____

_____

_____

Preventing problems (giving advice)? Which ones:

_____

_____

_____

_____

_____

_____

What do other people (prospective clients) not already know?

Make a list of your knowledge. Include education and experience. No need to be shy: brag away!

What is your unique perspective? What "common knowledge" do you have that others don't know?

_____

_____

_____

_____

_____

_____

_____

_____

What are your book ideas?

_____

_____

_____

_____

_____

_____

_____

_____

_____

Let's Eliminate Your Excuses

When will you make the time to write? Write down 5-10 possible times you can write (before work, during your commute, during lunch, after the kids go to bed). Get creative! You're worth it.

_____

_____

_____

_____

_____

_____

_____

_____

_____

_____

_____

_____

Where will your book manuscript live?

[ ] Microsoft Word [ ] Evernote [ ] Scrivener [ ] Other

Ninja Exercise:

What advice do I find myself giving over and over?

_____

_____

_____

_____

_____

_____

When someone has a problem in my area of knowledge, what problems are they asking me to help them solve?

_____

_____

_____

_____

_____

_____

What is the size of your target market, i.e., those who have a problem or problems you can solve with your knowledge, experience, and education?

_____

_____

_____

_____

_____

_____

CRAFTING YOUR BOOK

Identify what problem you're going to solve and/or what advice you're going to share.

I'm going to help my readers _____

_____

_____

_____

_____

For example: *I'm writing a book for professionals about how they can successfully self-publish a book, improve their brand, increase their authority, and their platform.*

Or, *I'm writing a book for people who have been through a divorce about how they can create a new life they love.*

I'm writing a book for

_____

about how they

_____ .

OBTAIN EFFECTIVE FEEDBACK.

It's a great idea to source qualified input about your book, from your intended target audience, other successful business book authors, and even Amazon (a fantastic search engine and resource for information).

SUCCESSFUL BUSINESS AUTHORS.

Who should I ask for feedback on my book idea:

_____

_____

_____

_____

_____

YOUR FAN CLUB [I.E., YOUR CLIENTS].

What are the questions most asked by your clients?

_____

_____

_____

_____

Another option is to create a survey and find out what your clients most want to know.

[ ] Craft a survey in Survey Monkey

THE 'ZON.

If one of your goals is to sell your book on Amazon (in ebook, paperback and/or audio formats), you'll want to make sure your book fits in *and* stands out. In other words, your book can, and should, have a similar look and feel to the bestselling books in your category (another reason to invest in a quality book cover designer).

Do a search on Amazon for books related to your topic. Identify a few you like, and make notes of their common elements. Write those title here:

_____

_____

_____

_____

_____

_____

_____

_____

_____

GETTING DOWN TO BUSINESS

It's time to begin working on your book!

Since publishing *You Must Write a Book*, I've had several questions about whether one can cobble together blog posts or use an already partially-written manuscript for their book. I will give you the standard lawyer's answer: *It depends.* (And no, I'm not a lawyer.)

While you *can* repurpose content into your book; however, I would not suggest taking blog posts, giving them a chapter each, and turning them into a book. Because you have defined what you want your reader to do (or not do, or both) because of reading your book, you can accurately pick and choose from any previously created content to see if it fits in with what your avatar needs to read.

Define Your Audience

Who is the audience for your book?

After crafting an outline, take the time to also do the following:

Create an avatar (a.k.a. ideal reader).

Imagine you have your ideal, most favorite, and wonderful client or customer sitting in front of you. You are giving them the advice they have asked for … you don't have any problem doing that, right? Of course not, because (drum roll please) *you're the expert!* If I asked you a question about financial planning, or forming a new entity, or how you handled office politics back in the 80s, you wouldn't hesitate; you would simply speak. When you define your avatar, keep in mind that in your book you are *giving advice to your favorite client.*

Before you start writing, list the qualities and characteristics of your ideal client. Describe the perfect person, couple, or company whose business would make you ecstatic. Use your very favorite client as an example. This will become your avatar. Here's an example, a short take on my ideal reader for this book. And yes, it's an actual person, one of my favorite clients:

<u>Eric Negron</u>

Financial Advisor, 10 years' experience

College educated, finance and economics degree

31 years of age

Married with three children

Homeowner

Mid-six-figure income, which he intends to multiple by three to four times

Accredited Wealth Management Advisor from College for Financial Planning

Focus: High Net-worth planning

Problem:

- **wants to multiply his business**
- **not considered "grey" enough**
- **needs more credibility with ultra-wealthy investors**

As I write about why you, my reader, should write and self-publish a book, I have Eric in mind. He's a long-time client and friend, and yes, we've had multiple conversations about why he should write a book. When you remember what your ideal client needs to hear, you will give targeted advice. My advice to Eric works perfectly as my advice to you and a wide range of other people. But an avatar focuses my thoughts. While your situation might be somewhat unique, 95 percent of the advice is applicable and is exactly what *you* need to write your book.

As a side note, I have a few other people in mind as well. But when it comes to giving actual advice, I think about what I want to tell Eric. It helps me make decisions to form the content ("Should I include this?") to the prose ("Is this the best way to describe this concept?").

IDENTIFY YOUR AVATAR HERE:

Name _____

Profession and experience _____

_____

Education _____

Age(s) _____

Marital status _____

Additional data as needed _____

_____

Problems/challenges:

Put as many problem/challenges here as necessary

- _____

- _____

- _____

- _____

- _____

- _____

If you are so inspired (and I suggest you are), write an additional paragraph or two about your avatar. This will help you make decisions about what to write about as you come to a fork in the road as you are writing, i.e., Should I talk about this or that? Well, what would you tell your avatar?

_____

_____

_____

_____

_____

_____

CREATE AN OUTLINE

Crafting your book will go more smoothly if you work from an outline. You'll write your desired daily word count, and reach your goal of having a book, much more easily with an outline that's solid and thought out.

Before I started writing *You Must Write a Book*, I crafted a rough outline. Here's the actual initial outline:

1. Why I wrote a book

2. Who should write a book

3. Why write an actual book

4. Why not a blog or newsletter, etc.

5. How to write

6. Getting it written

7. Publishing

8. Marketing the book

9. Who else has successfully written and self-published a business book?

As you can see, that's a pretty rough (and short) outline, and not much like the book looks today. I started with what I considered the easiest path to fleshing out an outline: using the *w* questions: who, what, where, when, and why ... and of course, the how. I suggest, at least initially, you use a similar process to flesh out your outline.

- ***Who* has the problem you can solve?**

_____

_____

_____

- ***What* do they need to do to avoid pain or gain pleasure, or both (i.e., what is your advice for them)?**

_____

_____

_____

- ***What* do they need to do, or avoid doing, to stay out of trouble, get out of trouble, or get the thing, event, or awesomeness they want?**

_____

_____

_____

- *Where* do they need to go, or avoid going, to get their desired result?

_____

_____

_____

- *When* do they need to take action?

_____

_____

_____

- *Why* must they do, or not do, what you're advising?

_____

_____

_____

- And, finally, *how* do they get what they want, or avoid what they don't want?

_____

_____

_____

This book, even as I write (and review) it, is still changing and expanding as I discuss it with my clients who are writing their books, my author friends, and even my editor. By the time you read these words, the final book will barely resemble the original outline. You can expect that your original idea will evolve into an expanded, even greater version, and this is a normal part of the process.

Once you have an initial outline, writing is going to be a breeze. Why do I say that? Because you're going to be writing about what you know!

A great place to start is with a mind map. I first learned about mind mapping from Tony Buzan (tonybuzan.com) in the mid-'90s from his book: *The Mind Map Book*. I loved (and still love) the way he suggests using a blank sheet of paper, some colored pencils or markers, and my imagination to flush out ideas, gain clarity, and provide direction.

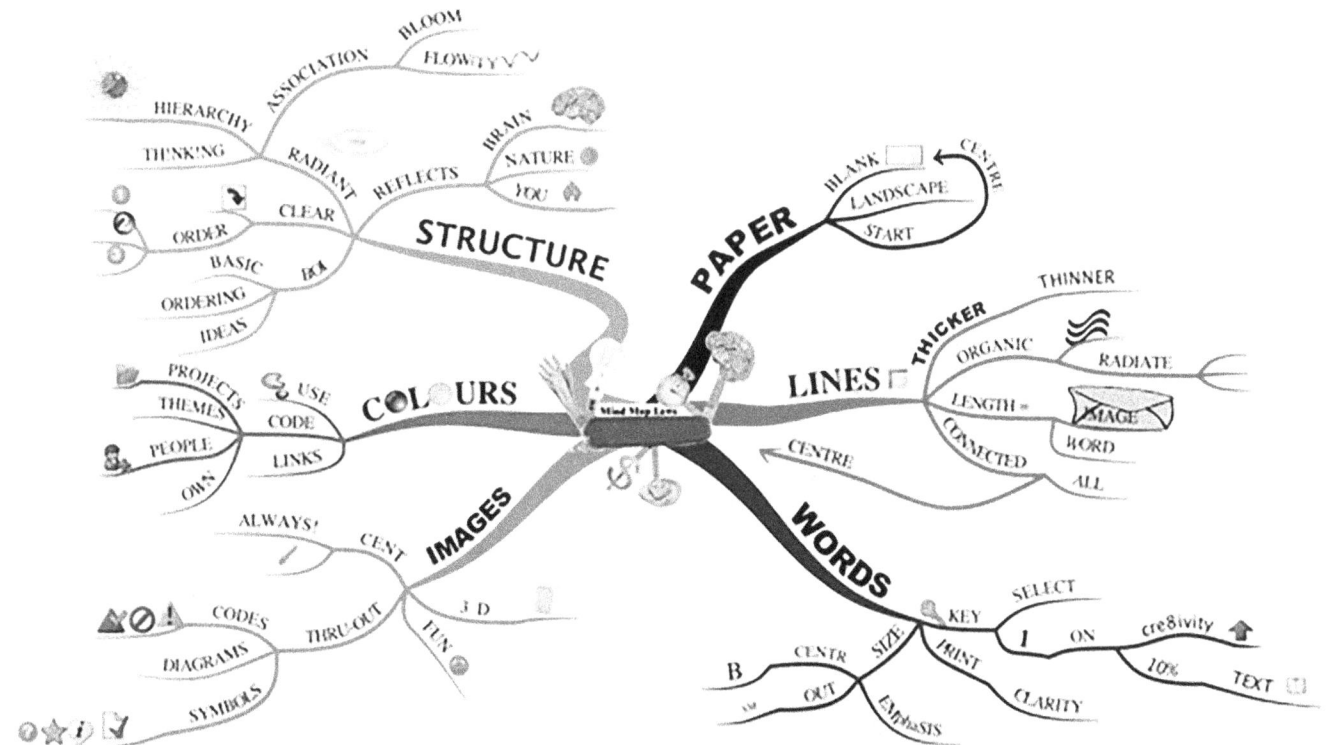

I've borrowed Tony's instructions for mind mapping from his website (TonyBuzan.com), and customized them for you:

1. **Start in the CENTRE of a blank page turned sideways.** Why? *Because starting in the center gives your Brain freedom to spread out in all directions and to express itself more freely and naturally.*

2. **Use an IMAGE or PICTURE for your central idea.** Why? *Because an image is worth a thousand words and helps you use your Imagination. A central image is more interesting, keeps you focused, helps you concentrate, and gives your Brain more of a buzz!*

3. **Use COLOURS throughout.** Why? *Because colors are as exciting to your Brain as are images. Colour adds extra vibrancy and life to your Mind Map, adds tremendous energy to your Creative Thinking, and is fun!*

4. **CONNECT your MAIN BRANCHES to the central image and connect your second- and third-level branches to the first and second levels, etc.** Why? *Because your Brain works by association. It likes to link two (or three, or four) things together. If you connect the branches, you will understand and remember a lot more easily.*

5. **Make your branches CURVED rather than straight-lined.** Why? *Because having nothing but straight lines is boring to your Brain.*

6. **Use ONE KEY WORD PER LINE.** Why? *Because single key words give your Mind Map more power and flexibility.*

7. **Use IMAGES throughout.** Why? *Because each image, like the central image, is also worth a thousand words.* So if you have only 10 images in your Mind Map, it's already the equal of 10,000 words of notes!

I've used mind mapping on a few occasions to get my creative juices flowing for a book project. You can use this process from the beginning, or you can use it when you become stuck in the outlining process. I've provided lined pages for your outline, and a couple of pages for mind mapping. I use Stabilo Point 88 markers (available on Amazon.com) for mind mapping, and I either use a blank sheet of paper, or I mind map in my Bullet Journal.

OUTLINE YOUR BOOK

1. Think of a tentative title that describes what you want to say, in a creative or highly effective way. You can always change it later, if necessary.
2. Brainstorm a list of key points you need to cover to address your overall message.
3. Jot a few notes under each of your key points, which you will later flesh out.

For example, when I wrote the blog post The 5 Components of a Bestseller (http://tinyurl.com/bestsellercomponents), I …

1. Gave it a descriptive title,
2. Decided on five key points to cover, and
3. Wrote one or two dot points under each key point to help me focus and keep on track as I filled in the meat of the article.

Of course, your first brief outline needs to be filled out until you can almost effortlessly write enough content to fill your book. Use my "W" questions and mind mapping to fully complete your outline. Once you have an initial outline, writing is going to be a breeze (I promise!). Why do I say that? Because you're going to be writing about what you know!

ADDITIONAL CONTENT IDEAS:

IDENTIFY YOUR MOST FREQUENTLY ASKED QUESTIONS.

What questions do new contacts or prospective clients frequently ask? What questions should they be asking? With just ten questions, you have enough to fill an entire book. Thirty questions? Three books! One hundred questions? You guessed it, ten books! In *The Successful Single Mom Book Series*, I answered the "big question" (how can a single mom become successful?) in the first book, and you can tell by each of these titles what questions I answered in the subsequent books:

*   *The Successful Single Mom Cooks! Cookbook*
*   *The Successful Single Mom Gets Rich*

- *The Successful Single Mom Finds Love*
- *The Successful Single Mom Gets Fit*
- *The Successful Single Mom Gets an Education*

SHARE STORIES.

There is truly nothing new under the sun, which mean your topic(s) has probably been written about before, *just not by you*. We find ourselves in the stories of others, so be sure to share your own stories, and the stories of previous clients (or others you've seen execute your advice successfully, or, alternatively, have paid the price of not having good advice).

WRITE NEW CONTENT, AND FEEL FREE TO REPURPOSE CONTENT.

Most likely, you have material you have previously created that can be used in your book. Think about any blog posts or articles you've written. Do you have a brochure? Have you delivered a speech, presentation, or workshop on your topic (and did they have notes, a power point, manual that accompanied it)? Did you write an article or do a guest blog post? Have you been interviewed on a podcast? These are great places to find content you can re-use, spark inspiration, or even inspire additional content.

I trust that this basic nonfiction outline template has given you enough juice to get started.

Book Outline #1

BOOK OUTLINE #2

Book Outline #3

MIND MAPPING

MIND MAPPING

MIND MAPPING

– 3 –

Choosing My Timeframe &

Creating My Action Plan

I conceived of the idea for *You Must Write a Book*, wrote it, had it edited, proofread, designed and published in 122 days. If I hadn't waited for external validation about my idea (see End of Book Stuff), that I would have shaved nine days off that total number. Using extreme focus, determination, a plan, and coordination with my incredible team, I found I could produce a quality book in what is ultimately an incredibly short period.

In case you're thinking *She's done this before, that isn't possible for me*, allow me to politely disagree. You have in your hands my exact process and access to just about everything I know. You *can* absolutely get your book done (and done well) in just about any timeframe you choose. Without further ado…

Let me dive into just three of your many options for writing your book, and you can choose the one that works best for you. Plus, now that you have an outline, you might feel more sure of your ability to get that book written (and if you haven't finished your outline, take some time to do that before proceeding).

Book Production Options

Based upon your set personal and professional obligations (and I realize you are already using every moment of your days), you can pick the track that works best for you. On each of the following three pages, you'll find three common tracks and the subsequent book production deadlines for each one. Based on the track you choose, you'll plug in the dates for when each piece of the book project is due.

Author's Note: When in doubt, choose the less aggressive track. It's better to be ready ahead of schedule than to stress when you fall behind schedule. It is almost impossible to make up time in the book publishing process, as you are relying on other professionals (whose schedules are already full as well). It costs additional fees to rush production, and even then, you might find yourself missing a deadline.

Holy Time-Warp Batman: 100 days

Holy Time-Warp Batman 100-day plan: Crafting, writing, and producing a book within 100 days is entirely possible. You will need to be intentional and purposeful with each move, schedule your team in advance (editor, proofreader, cover and interior design, and copywriter) and ruthlessly stick to your schedule.

To have a book 100 days from today, use my timeline below and create your schedule accordingly:

Timeline:

1. Final First Draft Outline Due (2 days)
2. First Rough Draft Due (allow 21 days)

3. Final First Draft Due (allow 14 days)

4. Send book to editor 1 (allow 8 days)

5. Review edits (allow 1 day)

6. Send book to proofreader (allow 4 days)

7. Send book to formatter (allow 10 business days)

8. Book to Street Team (2-3 weeks prior to Soft Launch)

9. Soft launch @ 99 cents (Friday before Hard Launch)

10. Hard launch (Monday or Tuesday)

11. Book party

Note: With this schedule, you'll need to schedule your editor and proofreader as soon as your outline is finished. This goes for your cover designer and interior layout designer as well. Any great editor/editing and design team will have limited availability of their schedule.

Faster-than-Normal 180-day plan

A more reasonable time-frame, perhaps, for the busy executive or entrepreneur. Six months might seem like a long time, but it will pass before you know it.

Timeline:

1. Final First Draft Outline Due (allow 14 days)

2. First Rough Draft Due (allow 60 days)

3. Final First Draft Due (allow 21 days)

4. Send book to editor 1 (allow 21 days)

5. Review edits (allow 7 days)

6. Send book to proofreader (allow 14 days)

7. Send book to formatter (allow 10 business days)

8. Send book to Street Team (2-3 weeks prior to Soft Launch)

9. Soft launch (Friday before Hard Launch)

10. Hard launch (Monday or Tuesday)

11. Book party

SLOW-AND-STEADY 365-DAY PLAN

The "just right" time-frame for you could be to write your book over the course of a year. That's terrific!

TIMELINE:

1. Outline Due (allow 30 days)

2. First Rough Draft Due (allow 150 days)

3. Final First Draft Due (allow 30 days)

4. Send book to editor 1 (allow 21 days)

5. Review edits (allow 7 days)

6. Send book to proofreader (allow 14 days)

7. Send book to formatter (allow 10 business days)

8. Send book to Street Team (2-3 weeks prior to Soft Launch)

9. Soft launch (Friday before Hard Launch)

10. Hard launch (Monday or Tuesday)

11. Book party

GOAL-SETTING:

You set some goals in Chapter 1 (check), you'll need them for your Action plan.

Determine the amount of money you want to make in the next year.

Your annual number is your Goal #1. _____.

Divide that number by 365. _____.

Your daily number is your Goal #2. _____.

CREATING AN ACTION PLAN

Regardless of the time-frame you choose to craft your book, you'll need a rock-solid action plan to help keep you on track. Following is a former client's example, and then a blank one for you to use (you can also download another blank version at HonoreeCorder.com/YouMustBonuses).

ACTION PLAN EXAMPLE

What I want from my book: *I am a full-time writer, earning in excess of $10,000 per month from my book and, as a result, $55,000 per month from my business.*

Goal #1: $120,000 2016 income = $10,000 per month

Goal #2: 95 total ebooks and print books sold per day

ACTION ITEMS:

1. Do 1 podcast interview every three days (122 total)

2. Add 5000 people to my email list (13.69 per day)

   • Update opt-in

   • Revise auto-responder sequence. You'll find an example at (yup, you guessed it): HonoreeCorder.com/YouMustBonuses, also in this Workbook in the next chapter.

   • Have twice daily updates in private Facebook group. (Use Bufferapp.com to schedule.)

   • Post on personal timeline four times per week

3. One blog post per week

4. Read top 100 other books in my genre, write reviews on Amazon and Goodreads.

5. Leave books/bookmarks/postcards in various locations (elevators, bookstores, etc.).

6. Write 2000 words per day in current work in progress to keep with my schedule to publish by [date].

Your Action Plan

What I want from my book: _____

_____

_____

Goal #1: $_____ income = $ _____ per month

Goal #2: _____ total ebooks and print books sold per day

Action Items:

1. _____

   _____

2. _____

   _____

3. _____

   _____

4. _____

   _____

5. _____

   _____

6. _____

   _____

Tip: Always identify action items for each goal the minute you set the goal. Then, pull out your calendar and schedule in times to complete those actions.

Reminder: It always takes longer, costs more, and requires more effort than we originally think to reach a goal ... and it is always worth it!

54

– 4 –

MULTIPLE STREAMS OF INCOME

I was first really exposed to repurposing content when I realized Tony Robbins' book *Awaken the Giant Within* ($15) was also a seminar (*Unleash the Power Within,* with a price tag at the time of $700), as well as an audio program (*Personal Power,* investment: $200). Based on his growing popularity, he also provided 1-on-1 coaching at $1 million per year (and certified coaches who charge much less). All of these products were based on the same core information.

Your book doesn't have to be "just" a book. In fact, it is a great idea to repurpose your content into other streams of income. I call these multiple streams of income the "Wheel of Fortune." As you can see, your book published on multiple platforms, and in different formats, as well as in different forms, can provide many different streams of income. Here are just eighteen:

THE WHEEL OF FORTUNE

1. Amazon Kindle
2. Amazon CreateSpace
3. Amazon Audible
4. Apple iBooks/iTunes
5. BarnesandNoble.com Nook
6. Kobo.com
7. Draft2Digital
8. Keynote speeches
9. Online courses
10. A workbook, journal, or companion guide
11. A workshop or training program
12. Weekend events
13. Professional services
14. Events
15. Merchandise
16. Coaching
17. Consulting
18. A mastermind group

You might want to do them all, but I think there are at least a few of them you will want to execute. Just not all at once, of course!

To start, pick 3-5 options for income streams:

_____

_____

_____

Next, make a to-do list for bringing your income streams to life:

– 5 –

Publishing Like a Pro

Quality is Paramount

You should remember this from *You Must Write a Book:*

> *The goal is to publish a book that is indistinguishable from traditional publishing.*

When you hold your book in your hands, and *more importantly*, when someone else holds your book in their hands, it is important (imperative, even!) your book represents you in the best possible way. Even as you are outlining your book, you need to be putting together your book production team.

There are four cornerstones of a professionally published book, in addition to amazing content, that need your focus and undivided attention: cover design, interior design, copywriting (also known as "sales copy," which you'll know as the back cover text and the book's description on your Amazon sales page), and editing with proofreading.

Form Your Book Team

Once you have broken ground on your book, you'll want to identify and hire your book team as soon as possible.

- **A book cover designer.** People really do judge a book by its cover. You will want to have a book cover that looks *fantastic*, one that compels people to pick it up and look at it. My amazing and talented cover designer is the one and only Dino Marino. You'll find him at DinoMarino.com and dino@DinoMarino.com. You can also source great covers at HonoreeCorder.com/99Designs.

   A couple of things to note: Do a search for best-selling books in your area of expertise and get a few examples of what sells. Provide them to your cover designer.

   - Expect to pay a *minimum* of $300 and upwards of $2,000 for a quality cover. The investment is worth it!

   - There are pages at the end of this chapter for you to paste your example book covers and final version.

- **A top-notch editor,** For information on my list of suggested editors, visit HonoreeCorder. com/YouMustBonuses.

- **A proofreader.** A proofreader does the final reading of a galley proof or an electronic copy of a publication to find and fix typos, production errors, and other mistakes. **Proofreaders** are expected to be consistently accurate by default because they occupy the last stage of book editing before publication.

Note: I categorize editing and proofreading together because you must have both. Very importantly, they shouldn't be the same person. There will be separate costs for both unless you use the same team/company.

- **An interior designer**. You can get custom book designs at a reasonable price, or for a little extra investment, you can add some special touches (such as customized fonts, chapter graphics, unique section markers, text graphics, graphs, boxes, etc.). My first choice for this is Dino Marino. In addition to preparing your book covers, he can also do a custom interior design of your book.

- **A copywriter.** Copywriting is its own animal. Unless you are a trained copywriter, you'll want to hire one to do your book's sales description. A well-written copy will compel the right people (remember your ideal reader avatar) to buy your book immediately.

See the following pages for two book descriptions before and after being worked on by an expert copywriter, courtesy of Bryan Cohen (professional copywriter and book description expert, author of *How to Write a Sizzling Synopsis*).

I've added a few lines for your notes about the differences.

_____

_____

_____

_____

_____

_____

_____

Book Description Comparison

Leadership Attributes for Women and Men

BEFORE:

Searching for good leaders?

Look within yourself.

This book will show you how.

The world is lacking leadership! Leadership where, what, how and why.

Leadership attributes that lie within each of us are the answer when leading in a disruptive world. Dr Vicky McGahey has 25 years' experience in the field of leadership as a practitioner and an academic.

The quest to be a good leader is a journey within. This book will guide you toward revealing your true potential to lead or just to be a better person.

Leadership is a quality, NOT a quantity. It can only truly be measured by the attributes of a person. Leadership is NOT something you do, it is who you are. Leadership is NOT a position, leadership is a choice.

You are NOT a leader without followers. First and foremost leadership is service. To do it well you need to lead with grace.

In this book you will discover the 15 Leadership Attributes. There are six key attributes and another nine orbital attributes that together can help women and men grow into the leaders that families, communities and organizations need in disruptive times.

There are stories of famous leaders, research findings, quotations, and questions to guide you as you discover the gift that is each attribute.

Buy the book to realise and release your potential to lead…or just to be a better person.

<u>Author's Note</u>: This isn't a *bad* description, but as you'll see, Bryan's expert touch takes it from "okay" to "terrific."

AFTER:

Want to improve your ability to lead, unlock your potential and transform the world?

Interested in stepping up as a leader in your organization? Do you want to break free from your follower mentality? Dr. Vicky McGahey is here to show you how.

With 25 years of leadership experience, McGahey has discovered 15 Leadership Attributes that all potential leaders possess. Through her extensive research findings, stories of famous leaders, and a series of mind-expanding questions, you'll finally learn how to reveal your true potential to lead.

In Leadership Attributes for Women and Men, you'll discover:

- How the attributes for leadership are already a part of who you are
- How to take advantage of transformational learning experiences to grow as a leader
- How to best provide your service to families, communities, and organizations
- How to once and for all make the choice to become a leader
- How to help others see leadership qualities in themselves, and much, much more!

When you learn that leadership isn't a quantity you memorize, but a quality you must embody, you'll become a better leader and a stronger person. McGahey's insightful, timely book will empower you to lead in any industry or organization.

Through the book's wise words, you'll start the necessary changes within that will not only change you, but the world around you as well. The world is lacking leadership. It's time to take your rightful place at the top.

Buy the book to reach your true potential today!

Author's Note: See what I mean? Yup, it's worth it to invest the $200-$300 to have a professional make your book description, also your sales copy, *fantastic!*

PLACE YOUR DRAFT BOOK COVER HERE:

PLACE YOUR FINAL BOOK COVER HERE:

72

– 6 –

Titling, Selling, &

Protecting My Book

Section I:
Things to Consider and Decide

The title and subtitle of your book can greatly impact your book's sales. I cover this in-depth in *You Must Write a Book*, so be sure to review that section and carefully determine your book's final title and subtitle.

YOUR TITLE

Keep in mind your title is the "what."

What is the book about?

_____

_____

_____

_____

What is the *working* title of your book:

_____

_____

_____

_____

What is the final title of your book:

_____

_____

Your Subtitle is the Promise

What does your book *promise*? What will your reader take away from reading your book? How will they benefit from taking your advice? Will they save money? Make money? Set themselves up for success?

What are the promises of your book:

_____

_____

_____

_____

_____

_____

_____

What is your *working* subtitle?

_____

_____

_____

What is the final subtitle of your book:

_____

_____

_____

Your Keywords

The keywords you choose are critical to your book's success. Choosing the right keywords are important for an author to get their books found by Amazon shoppers. Keywords are the words they type into Amazon's search bar when they are looking for their next book, or a book on a specific topic. My friend Dave Chesson created a tool to expedite the process of identifying the best keywords for your book called Publisher Rocket. Publisher Rocket will help you find the exact phrases shoppers type into Amazon when searching for a book on your topic (and even tell you how many people use that phrase when buying their next book). Find out more here: http://tinyurl.com/PublisherRocket.

What are the keywords for your book:

_____

_____

_____

_____

_____

_____

PRICING YOUR BOOK

How you price your book will be based upon several factors: (a) how other books in your area of expertise are priced, (b) how long it has been on the market, (c) the size of your platform, and (d) how excited your market is to get their hands on the information.

What are the titles and prices of the top 20 books in your preferred category?

_____

_____

_____

_____

_____

_____

_____

_____

_____

_____

_____

_____

_____

PLATFORMS FOR PUBLISHING

As of this writing, I strongly suggest you publish on Amazon initially (ebook, paperback, and if possible, audiobook), and enroll in KDP Select for at least the first 90 days after publication.

It is also wise to go ahead and set up accounts at the other online retailer locations (it is easier to set them all up at once since you'll be inputting the same information over and over).

WHERE YOU PUBLISH YOUR BOOKS

- Amazon
- Kindle Direct Publishing (KDP)
- ACX (a.k.a. Audible, a channel for audiobooks)
- Apple's iBooks (https://www.apple.com/itunes)
- Barnes and Noble's Nook (http://www.nookpress.com)
- Kobo (https://www.kobo.com/writinglife)
- Draft2Digital (they distribute to all of the major online distribution channels, including libraries; https://www.draft2digital.com)

PROTECT YOURSELF AND YOUR INTELLECTUAL PROPERTY

At the very least, read the section in _You Must Write a Book_ about how to protect yourself and your book. At the most, consult your business attorney and a separate intellectual property attorney to make sure everything is in order.

Making the right moves with your intellectual property will provide peace of mind down the road, especially if your book creates huge streams of direct and indirect income.

Who is your Corporate Attorney (include contact info)?

_____

_____

Who is your Intellect Property Attorney (include contact info)?

_____

_____

What steps do you need to take to protect your book, your business, and yourself?

_____

_____

_____

_____

_____

_____

_____

ꜩ

SECTION II:
Actions to Take

BOOK PUBLISHING CHECKLIST

by Honorée Corder

Your Title:_____

_____

Subtitle: _____

_____

Timeline:

_____ **Outline Due**

_____ **First Rough Draft Due**

_____ **Final First Draft Due**

_____ **Send book to editor 1 (allow 2-3 weeks)**

_____ **Review edits (allow 2-3 days)**

_____ **Send book to proofreader (allow 1-2 weeks)**

_____ **Send book to formatter (allow 10 business days)**

_____ **Book to Street Team (2-3 weeks prior to Soft Launch)**

_____ **Soft launch @ 99 cents (Friday before Hard Launch)**

_____ **Hard launch (Monday or Tuesday)**

_____ **Book party**

Book Contents:

☐ **Identify working title {the what}:** _____

_____

_____

☐ **Identify subtitle {the promise/hook} for your book:** _____

_____

_____

   ☐ **Promises for the book**

      o _____

_____

o _____

_____

o _____

_____

☐ **Keywords**

1. _____

2. _____

3. _____

4. _____

5. _____

6. _____

7. _____

☐ **Interviews (if applicable)**

☐ **Foreword**

o Who? _____

o Received by (prior to editing):_____

Technical:

▶ *Complete these items while you're still in the first rough draft stage.*

☐ **Commission a cover:** _____

    ☐ Front cover (ebooks)

    ☐ Full cover pdf (paperback/hardback)

    ☐ Audiobook

  > **Get an ISBN (myidentifiers.com)**

    o Ebook

    o Paperback

    o Hardcover

  > **Get Barcode (myidentifiers)**

    o Paperback _____

    o Hardcover _____

      Note: have your designer review KDP & CreateSpace & ACX requirements

▶ **Create accounts on:**
    ☐ Amazon ebook (KDP.com)

    ☐ Amazon paperback (CreateSpace)

    ☐ Audible (ACX.com)

    ☐ iBooks (Apple ebooks; https://support.apple.com)

☐ Kobo (kobo.com)

☐ Barnes and Noble

▶ **Create New Titles on:**

☐ KDP

☐ Audible (ACX.com, a division of Amazon, also distributes simultaneously to iTunes)

☐ iBooks (Apple ebooks; https://support.apple.com/; requires an Apple computer)

☐ Kobo (kobo.com)

☐ BarnesandNoble.com

▶ **Set book prices:**

☐ Ebook _____

☐ Paperback _____

☐ Hardcover _____

> Set prices according to other books in your genre

> Audible prices are set automatically by Audible based upon the genre and length of the finished audiobook

☐ **Send the final version to a book formatter for:**

o .mobi file (Amazon KDP)

o .epub (iBooks, Kobo, and all other platforms)

o PDF

o Print (paperback/hardcover layout)

o 2-free chapter (for download/list-building purposes)

☐ **Commission/record audio version by date:**

- o Deadline for first 15 minutes*:_____

- o Deadline for final audiobook*:_____

- \> You can hire a great narrator to read your book and pay them by the finished hour, or you can do a joint agreement in ACX where narrators audition to record your book, there is no up-front investment, and profits are split 50/50 for 7 years.

☐ **Add front and back matter to books:**

- o Copyright page (front)

- o List of other publications (front)

- o Acknowledgments (front)

- o Bio page (back)

- o Author's notes (back)

- o CTA (Call to Action) (back)

  - \> TBD

- o Optional (back):

  - \> Glossary

  - \> Index

  - \> Reference materials

Marketing/Promotion:

☐ **Hire copywriter for the sales description/back cover matter:**

- o Bryan Cohen: BestPageForward.net

- o Kevin Tumlinson is another terrific option: Kevin@Tumlinson.net.

☐ **Goal: 300-500 on Advanced Review Team**

- o Announce Call for Advanced Review Team on Facebook

  - ▪ Form private Facebook group

  - ▪ Date: _____ (30 days prior to launch)

- o Send book to Advanced Review Team (via BookFunnel.com)

  - ▪ Date: _____ (14-21 days prior to launch)

☐ **Goal: 100 *verified* reviews on launch day**

- o Actual number of reviews on Launch Day: _____

☐ **Promote your free offer/lead magnet (2-chapter opt-in)**

- o What: 2-chapter opt-in

- o What else? : _____

- o When: _____ (during soft launch)

- o Where/How? (Email or social media)

☐ **Set dates for email list promo:**

- • Tease: _____

  (the book is coming in 7 days)

- • It's here: _____

  (the book is here!)

☐ **Create advertising tracking codes.**

o Join *Amazon Affiliates* (affiliate-program.amazon.com)

> This is an optional but beautiful additional way to make money from your book and other things that are purchased on Amazon.

☐ **Create an account on MailChimp or Aweber**

o Create follow-up campaign

o Study AutoResponder Madness

o Build your list to 2500 prior to book launch

☐ **Leverage other people's platforms:**

o **Podcasts**

- Search for podcasts (radio shows) related to your subject matter

- Review Honorée's email request to appear on podcast; customize it to you and your book(s)

- Review Honorée's One-Pager Interview Sheet

- Have a professional headshot to provide to podcasts

- Schedule radio shows/podcasts for <30 days from launch date

o **Blogs**

- Write related subject matter posts

- Search for blogs who are related to your book's subject matter

- Offer to provide your posts to those blogs in exchange for the ability to provide a by-line that mentions your website and your book.

☐ **Create an Amazon Author Profile**

☐ **Add book to your Amazon Author Profiles**

☐ **Create Author Profile on BookBub.com**

Post-Launch/Review:

☐ **Evaluate launch campaign.**

☐ **Start the next book!**

☐ **Analyze options to create multiple streams of income from this book:**

- o Coaching

- o Course

- o Workbook

- o Consulting

- o Other: _____

- o Other: _____

o Other: _____

o Other: _____

o Other: _____

o Other: _____

– 7 –

My Book Launch

Book Launch Strategy

There are many ways to launch a book. As of the writing of *You Must Write a Book*, the most common launch strategy was to do a pre-sale and launch at 99 cents. Set it up for pre-sale, get busy promoting it, and you will want to …

Set a Date and Tell the World

The moment you have filled in the dates on your Book Publishing Checklist, announce to the world "I have a book in the works!" Of course, I advise you to be as certain as you can possibly be about the date. Barring any unforeseen circumstances, your intended publication date should be your actual publication date. I highly suggest you read *Sell More Books with Less Social Media* by Chris Syme, which was not available when I wrote *You Must Write a Book*. It contains absolute gold when it comes to social media strategy and can help you to do much more with much less.

Target Publication Date:_____

Give Yourself a Hashtag

The hashtag you assign to your book could be your book's title, the subtitle, or a key phrase out of the book. I chose to use #youmustwriteabook and #businessdating for two of my books of the same titles. With every Facebook post, tweet, or Instagram photo, you'll use your hashtag so that in the event someone searches for the hashtag on any social media platform; they will be able to find not only your posts, but also posts by other fans and followers.

Pick a hashtag for your first book, and if you get the bug, there's space for your future book's hashtags, too…

Book 1 Hashtag: #_____

Book 2 Hashtag: #_____

Book 3 Hashtag: #_____

Book 4 Hashtag: #_____

Book 5 Hashtag: #_____

Book 6 Hashtag: #_____

Book 7 Hashtag: #_____

Book 8 Hashtag: #_____

Book 9 Hashtag: #_____

Book 10 Hashtag: #_____

All of the Formats

I advise you publish your book in at least three of the four available formats: ebook, paperback, audiobook, and hardcover. I say this for multiple reasons: first, it looks very professional (and you are a professional, after all) to have multiple formats available on your book sales pages. Second, everyone has a different way they like to consume content. I like having every single book on my iPad and/or Kindle for when I'm traveling. I like having audiobooks for when I'm driving, working out, or doing "chores." (I hate chores, but I'll happily do them when I'm engrossed in a great book.)

For a while, I bought into the rumor that print was dead, and only published ebooks. But there are still lots and lots (and lots!) of readers who like to buy print versions to use as reference material, they like to "touch" the book, make notes and highlight in it, and to easily go back and forth between pages. It was quite a bit of work to create print versions for my backlist, but it's been worth it. From the beginning, I suggest you do the little bit extra it takes to create a print book.

Hardcover books are in their own category, none of my books to date are in hardcover. I plan to do a collector's edition of one of my books someday, and that will be in hardcover.

Select which versions you plan to publish:

- ☐ Ebook
- ☐ Paperback
- ☐ Audiobook
- ☐ Hardcover (optional)

SUGGESTED TACTICS FOR YOUR BOOK LAUNCH

CREATE A PRE-ORDER PAGE FIFTEEN TO NINETY DAYS PRIOR TO LAUNCH.

Amazon, iBooks, and most other platforms allow for pre-orders (for ebooks only, as of this writing) up to ninety days prior to your release date. Assuming selling books online is part of your strategy, having your book available for pre-sale is a great way to build buzz and even begin prospective client conversations.

For your pre-order, you'll need:

- ☐ The working draft of your manuscript to upload

- ☐ Your front book cover image

- ☐ Your book description

- ☐ Title, subtitle

- ☐ Keywords

- ☐ Pricing for all U.S. and foreign markets

CONTACT BOOKBUB & BUCKBOOKS.NET FOR A PROMOTION.

BUILD YOUR EMAIL LIST WITH A LEAD MAGNET.

- Decide on your lead magnet (such as two free chapters or another downloadable). See list, below.

- Sign up for an email service. I recommend Aweber (http://www.aweber.com/?436440), or you could use Infusionsoft or even MailChimp.

  - Go through your Rolodex, email contacts, and phone, and send an email requesting that people opt in to your list. I use a double opt-in, which requires subscribers to confirm they want to be on my list.

  - If you aren't already, start regularly communicating with your list.

23 Lead Magnet Ideas

1. A different ebook than the one you're selling

2. A guide or workbook that enriches your book's reader

3. The audiobook version of your book

4. A two-chapter excerpt of the book

5. Two-chapter excerpt of a different book

6. An article that pertains to the content of the book, but is not included

7. Sneak preview of an upcoming book

8. Notes from an interview you conducted to write the book

9. Bonus material you discuss in the book

10. A boxed set of two or more of your other books

11. A behind-the-scenes look at your writing process

12. A YouTube video of you speaking in-depth about your book or area of expertise

13. Exclusive, never-before-published content

14. Promotion or discount codes for a different product or service

15. A PDF of a resource list, checklist, worksheet, journal, or workbook

16. Access to a course that accompanies the book

17. Entry into a contest or giveaway

18. Subscription to your newsletter

19. Access to a free or low-cost training

20. A free consultation or a discount on a consultation

21. A recorded coaching/consulting call, interview, or the video of a keynote speech

22. Free VIP membership

23. One month free access to a monthly subscription

Choose Your Lead Magnets:

_____

_____

_____

_____

Email your list about your book:

☐ Seven days prior to launch _____

☐ Day of launch _____

☐ A week or two after the launch _____

Leverage friends, contact, and network.

If you've read my book *Business Dating*, or even *How to Win Friends and Influence People*, then you have a deep well of people to draw from, ask for favors and help with your book launch. I suggest the following:

☐ Make a list of influencers with whom you are more friends than friendly.

☐ Ask if they will share about your book in an email, or even as a post on social media.

☐ If you belong to clubs, organizations, or associations, see if you can:

> Do a presentation to the membership

> Advertise or get a mention in their newsletter, email blast, or on their social media

> Provide copies to the leadership

> Get creative and come up with your own distribution and marketing ideas:

_____

_____

_____

_____

_____

CREATE SHAREABLE SOCIAL MEDIA IMAGES AND POSTS.

Your graphic/cover designer can use your cover as the inspiration for creating social media graphics in different shapes.

- The front cover image can be expanded to create an oblong header for a Facebook group.

- The same square image you use for your audiobook cover can be used as your personal Facebook page image (a.k.a. your profile picture), on Instagram as a post, or even your profile photo.

- ClickToTweet.com to help your advance reader team, fans, and followers help spread the word. Here's an example:

> This is your year to become a full-time, prosperous writer!
> #ProsperityforWriters http://amzn.to/28Zdo0Z.

{Here's the Click-to-Tweet link for the text: http://ctt.ec/5Aqob.}

Amazon Marketing Services Advertising Campaigns

Amazon.com has been a leader in allowing anyone to get their message out through self-publishing. Check out their advertising options at https://ams.amazon.com/.

Facebook Ads

Facebook allows for very specific ad targeting (so targeted, you could craft an ad that only your next-door neighbor would get). You can spend a lot of money and get very little to no return if you don't know what you're doing. Mark Dawson provides a course called *Facebook Ads for Authors*. You can find out more about it here: http://www.selfpublishingformula.com/facebook-advertising-for-authors/. (I have no affiliation with Mark, but I have his course, and it's brilliant.)

Form a Private, Topic-Specific Facebook Group

My private Facebook Group, the Prosperity for Writers Mastermind, is where I hang out most of the time on Facebook. A group that you lead, which will eventually become your tribe, is a free way to build name, face, and brand recognition where people are already hanging out.

Come up with a name for your group (I love Hal Elrod's Miracle Morning Community, as well as Pat Flynn's group, Pat's First Kindle Book (from start to finish)). Come up with the name, establish your own personal rules in a pinned post, and start inviting people. Be sure to visit a couple of times daily, start discussions, and provide value to your members. You'll love it when people are active on their own, start discussions, and provide value!

My group name:_____

Goodreads

Goodreads is where *readers* hang out. It has been said a four-star review on Goodreads is equivalent to a five-star review on Amazon and I have found that to be true myself. Be sure to:

- ☐ Set up an author profile.

- ☐ Claim your book(s) on Goodreads.

☐ Do a Goodreads Giveaway (digital or physical copy). I do one or more a month.

☐ Read this article on getting the most out of Goodreads: http://www.authormedia.com/how-to-promote-books-goodreads/

Use a Pre-Launch Team, Your "ART," to Spread the Word

Creating and cultivating your ART (Advance Review Team) is an art. Here are your steps for executing a launch team like a pro:

1. **Recruit.** Recruit members onto your ART.

    Key tip: Recruit only individuals who are also your avatar. This will come in handy later when they buy and review your book on Amazon. Amazon uses metadata to target other readers like the ones who have read and enjoyed your book.

2. **Send regular updates.** You don't need to email them daily or even weekly, but keeping them in the loop about your process and how soon they can expect to receive your book to read (and your expectations for them) is good ART management.

3. **Send the book.** Create an account on, and utilize BookFunnel (http://bookfunnel.com) to distribute your books. It is hassle free, practically free to use, and I cannot recommend it enough. Two to three weeks prior to the official launch of your book, give the book to your ART.

4. **Ask your ART to read it as soon as possible.** When you deliver the link for the book, tell them the launch date of the book, ask them to read the book as soon as possible and send *you* their review. Plan to send a reminder to your entire ART every day or two prior to the launch. On the eve of your launch, have your assistant send them back their review with a link to your book, and ask them to take just 90 seconds to buy and review the book.

    Note: *Verified reviews* hold much more weight. A verified review is determined by whether someone has purchased the book.

5. **Capture the best of the book.** Start a thread in your ART Facebook group and ask the members to leave their favorite quotes and ideas there.

6. Continue to cultivate your ART. Here's a complete list of action steps:

   a. Post daily videos.

   b. Send those videos by email to the list.

   c. Give resources to share.

   d. Start threads at least once a day.

   e. Give encouragement, celebrate special moments, and be positive whenever you can.

   f. Make it easy for them to share your message by providing tweets and photo posts.

   g. Ask them to change their Facebook photo to a square graphic of your book for the day.

7. Launch! On launch day, thank your ART for reading, hopefully purchasing and reviewing your book. Remind them a couple of days later, thanking those who have left their reviews … and perhaps a few days later, the same type of email: {insert email}

_____

_____

_____

_____

_____

LAUNCH PRICING STRATEGY

Note: *This is my pricing strategy as of this writing. It changes slightly with every book launch.*

- Three days before your hard launch is the date of your soft launch. (1) Pricing your book at $0.99.

- Raise your price to $2.99 on your official launch day, and leave it there for about three days.

- Raise your book's price to between $3.99 and $5.99 on days seven through ten. Use your Amazon ranking to determine if the price should be raised or not.
- If you are still selling a fair number of books (20–25 or more a day), even as you raise the price, you can continue to raise it at regular intervals until you've hit your pre-determined full retail price.

The launch phase of your book starts from the moment you declare you're writing a book until about forty-five days post-launch. Keep in mind, this is only the beginning! The real work continues on day forty-five and beyond.

– 8 –

Marketing My Book

The real fun begins after the launch of your book. Beginning about forty-five days after your book's launch (assuming you're using online retail platforms to sell your book), you will benefit the most from planning to market your book with consistency for at least the next seventy-five years. If you are simply using your book to market your business, you might be tempted to jump into the next chapter. There are a few of the strategies from this chapter that will help you achieve your goals, so at least give it a "once-over."

Best Book Marketing Strategies: Awesome Ways to Find Book Buyers, Readers, and Raise Your Profile

Connecting with book buyers and readers will help you to accomplish the goals you've set for your book. Making your book easy to find will allow prospective readers, and ultimately prospect clients, to stumble upon your book and perhaps determine you're the very person they've been looking to find!

Use a Free Two-Chapter Opt-in

I suggest using the front and back matter of your book (title page, table of content, introduction, Foreword, bio, etc.) along with your first two chapters as a lead magnet and to allow prospective readers (and prospects) to get a sense of you and your book without a purchase.

The reason this is terrific is because it will add people to your email list. This means you can market to them consistently (which will help you both determine if you are a good fit for further work together).

☐ Create a two-chapter opt-in.

☐ Create a landing page on website.

☐ Create a thank you page on website.

☐ Draft an email auto-responder series:

- Thank you, here is your free sample (include a link to buy the book).

- Second email with link, reminding them to read it.

- Third email asking if they have any questions, or would they like to schedule a quick call or coffee.

☐ Add a link to your opt-in to your email signature. (See example, below.)

☐ Craft a social media post with book cover: *Get two free chapters of my book Business Dating here: HonoreeCorder.com/BusinessDatingsample.*

Add a Link to Your Email Signature

> **Honorée Corder**
>
> *Author, Speaker, Coach*
>
> Have you read my new book, *You Must Write a Book?* Get two free chapters <u>here</u> and buy it <u>here</u>.
>
> (Hyperlink the first "here" with a link to your 2-chapter opt-in, and the second "here" to your book on an online retailer or your book's website page.)

Make the Ask

If you don't a-s-k, you don't g-e-t. Reaching out to your network, letting them know you have a book, and asking if they would like one is *the fastest way to get the word out about your book*. I suggest you actually pick up the phone and give 'em a call. Yes, you might have five hundred, or even five thousand people to connect with. That's great! Settle on a number to call every day, and start smiling and dialing.

Note: If you only have a couple of dozen people to reach out to, that's fine, too. The great thing about a book is you now have a reason to reach out to people you don't know at all. Order 50 books, and call people until you've given them all away.

Here's the strategy, broken down into key steps:

1. Make a list of your best business relationships and call them one by one.

2. Tell them you have a new book and ask if they would like a complimentary copy. Be willing to give them a book to review first. In fact, if the relationship is deep enough, some of those on your list might be a great candidate for your ART.

3. Ask if they want a digital or paperback copy and immediately send them the book. It's a great idea to use an Excel spreadsheet to track this.

4. Follow up in three weeks to ask if they've had a chance to read the book. If yes, ask the magic question, "Would you like to buy between 10 and 100 books?" If no, tell them you'll be back in touch soon. Wait another three weeks. Rinse and repeat.
A couple of things to consider:

- Your approach here is to find out if there are other people your contact knows who would benefit from having the information contained in the book. It might help *their* business to share your book. They might think it would be beneficial to the relationship they have with you by sharing your book.

- You can offer them a discount, or even to provide the books at your cost (I recommend at least $5 per book to cover actual costs plus administrative and delivery/shipping costs).

- It is your job to ask the question; it's up to them whether or not they want to buy more or multiple copies. Just ask. I promise you: no professionals were ever killed in the process of asking.

Become a Podcast Guest

Podcasts are the magic bullet of book marketing for professionals. You must get the word out about how awesome of a professional you are … and, like the star you are, you've put a nice portion of your business knowledge into a convenient-sized package, easily digested by all (your book). Podcasts always need new guests, and if you serve the podcasters target market, chances are they will jump at the chance to interview you. In addition to your book, being interviewed *as the expert* means you are now the expert.

The best news about podcasts is they are evergreen. While the actual listenership of a podcast can range from a few to a few million, I don't discriminate based on listenership because I can share my interview with my email list. This provides a win-win-win: your connections learn about a new podcast they just might like, the podcast gains new listeners, and you will possibly either sell a book, gain a new client, or both.

Here's your process to podcast guest super stardom:

1. Identify podcasts with the same target audience as your book and expertise.

2. Send an email introduction, telling the host who you are and what you have to offer their audience.

PODCAST REQUEST EMAIL TEMPLATE

Hello, _____!

I work with (or I am, but your assistant should handle this) _____, he/she is _____ (insert professional title) and I think he/she would be an excellent guest on your podcast! Say something short and sweet about what's going on with your business.

In this paragraph, share a couple sentences about your experience and professional knowledge. Describe the book and use a few examples of topics that would interest the show's listeners.

You can find more information about _____ here (insert website link) and you can view other interviews on similar podcasts like list podcast names here. Note: If you do not have podcast examples, share any recorded interviews, blog links, articles and additional information you'd like the podcast show host to know.

Thank you for your time,

Signature Here

HONORÉE'S EXAMPLE

Hello, _____!

I work with Honorée Corder, bestselling author and book coach, and I think she would be an excellent guest on your podcast! Her most recent release, *The Miracle Morning for Writers*, with coauthors Hal Elrod and Steve Scott, is already a bestseller on Amazon!

Honorée has almost 20 years of writing and coaching experience and she now provides structure and strategy to individuals who want to elevate their platform and create multiple streams of income from their writing. She has numerous topics that may interest your listeners: daily writing strategies of successful authors, creating an abundance mindset, making your book a business, and step-by-step help for self-publishing.

You can find out more about Honorée here (provide a link to your bio or LinkedIn profile) and you can view other interviews on similar podcasts like The Author Strong Podcast, The Author Hangout, Authority Self-Publishing podcast, Eight Questions - Sterling & Stone, Eventual Millionaire, and the Wordslinger Podcast. (Don't worry if you don't yet have any interviews to share. Just leave this sentence out until you do.)

Thank you so much for your time, and I look forward to hearing your thoughts!

Your Assistant's Name & Title

My Assistant's Two Cents [worth at least $1,000,000 in potential revenue]:

I always try to tailor each podcast request to the show's mission statement. Read through the show's description on iTunes and get a solid idea of what their listeners may want. The example above is only one example of the podcast requests we send out. Each is different based on what's going on in the business and book releases. The most important thing to remember is to keep it short, sweet, and to the point. Grab their attention, let them know how to get more information and reach back out to you. I think you're ready! Happy podcast hunting!

• When the host expresses interest, provide them with your bio, headshot, and interview sheet. Download a Word version to customize here: HonoreeCorder.com/YouMustBonuses.

• A few other quick pointers:

  > Be your authentic self on interviews. You have expertise that others want. Share as much as you can as openly as you can.

  > Have a great microphone. I suggest the Logitech ClearChat Comfort/USB Headset H390, which is affordable (less than $30 on Amazon), comfortable, and works very well.

  > Be sure to mention your book (and ask the host to do the same in the introduction and as they close the show).

  > Have a URL you share on every show, such as HonoreeCorder.com/Writers.

Offer Bloggers Advance Reader Copies

Search for bloggers in your area of expertise or ones who speak to those in your target audience. Members of their audience doesn't have to be your exact avatar (see the example, below). Call or send an email offering a complimentary copy of your book and ask if they would be willing to write a blog post about it. Mail with a handwritten note, thanking them for taking the time to read and review. Follow-up three to four weeks later.

Here is an example: http://buff.ly/2hhXrq8. Judson Moore is a travel blogger, and yet he reviewed *You Must Write a Book*. Why? Because he wants to write a book, and because he knows his readers do, also.

Make a list of bloggers here:

_____

_____

_____

_____

_____

_____

_____

_____

_____

_____

_____

_____

_____

_____

_____

_____

BECOME A HARO SOURCE

Helpareporter.com was founded by Peter Shankman a dozen years ago to create a bridge between sources and reporters. In its present form, everyone from "legit" media (well-known newspapers, magazines, and television shows) to bloggers or authors looking for sources are members of HARO. Subscribe to HARO's emails and regularly check to see if someone is requesting information in your area of expertise. You can receive up to three emails every single day with great opportunities to get the message out about your expertise, products and/or services.

☐ Subscribe to HARO

ADD YOUR BOOK TO YOUR LINKEDIN PROFILE

Once your book is published, be sure to add information about your book to your LinkedIn profile. Click **+Add Publication** and fill in the title, subtitle, book description, author(s), and publication date. The update will show up in the LinkedIn timeline, and from then on, your book will be what people see when they view your profile!

☐ Add your book to your LinkedIn Profile

SPEAKING OF LINKEDIN ...

Maximizing your LinkedIn profile is one way to market your book (and therefore, yourself). Here are several ways to round out your profile and help it to work for you:

1. Set up a complete profile. The basic idea here is to not leave any gaps. Fill in each section, using the Profile Strength Indicator as a guide (your goal is "all-star").

2. Have a professional photo *and* include your book cover image.

3. Connect with the right people. Connect with other business authors, other high-profile individuals in your field, and of course, all your past and current clients.

4. Collect endorsements and recommendations.

5. Participate in a special interest group. Groups on LinkedIn are a terrific place to interact with key players in your industry, which will help you to make more connections (see #3) and become an influencer.

Capitalize on Holidays Corresponding with Your Book

Identify holidays (or create holidays) you can use to promote your book:

☐ _____

☐ _____

☐ _____

☐ _____

☐ _____

☐ _____

☐ _____

☐ _____

☐ _____

☐ _____

☐ _____

☐ _____

☐ _____

☐ _____

☐ _____

☐ _____

☐ _____

☐ _____

Public Relations

Be sure to read the interview I shared with Gabrielle Torello of Grande Communications in *You Must Write a Book*. Very few authors can afford a PR firm with enough juice to put their books on the map. Your best bet is to formulate your own PR campaign.

Something new since *You Must Write a Book* was released: a fantastic new book by Chris Syme: *Sell More Books with Less Social Media*. I dare say you won't want to worry about traditional PR at all once you get your hands on this book and the amazing free course that accompanies it!

– 9 –

Marketing with My Book

For the rest of your career (and life), you can (and must!) market your business with your book. What follows is a menu of marketing ideas you can use and customize to suit you.

Best "Marketing with My Book" Strategies

A subtle difference from book marketing strategies, this set of suggestions centers solely on using your book to generate new business and/or sales.

HAVE A BOOK HANDY, ALWAYS.

Keep a book on or near you *always*. Keep several in your office, each car you own, and at home.

Three tricks I've uncovered:

1. Take the time to autograph all your books. Also, keep a sharpie with one of your book's colors handy. *You Must Write a Book*'s signature color is red, so of course, I had to buy a half-dozen red sharpies with which to sign my book. *smile*

2. Place a business card inside the front cover.

3. Keep manila envelopes and labels handy so you can quickly mail a book upon request.

Speaking of the mail ... When you meet someone new, and you get their business card, offer to send them a book if you don't have one handy. Get the person's mailing address and send them a signed and autographed book. Be sure to follow-up in a week or two to ensure they've received it. Your call or email will serve as a gentle nudge for them to read the book.

GIVE THAT PUPPY AWAY LIKE IT'S CANDY.

When in doubt, give your book away. Even if the recipient doesn't find it useful, they will most likely pass it on to someone who will. Come on, it's only a few bucks and this particular piece of great karma can and will come back to you in spades.

SIGNING VS. AUTOGRAPHING.

When you give the book to someone, ask them if they'd like it signed. Usually, they do. Sometimes, they want it made out to someone else to give as a gift. Signing and autographing are different—an autograph is just your signature on the title page; signing is when you add a personal message from you to the (intended) recipient.

Tip: Have a standard phrase based upon your book's topic to use when signing your book, such as: *It's time to turn your Vision to Reality* or *Your divorce is your new beginning!* or *I can't wait to read your book!* That way, when it comes time to sign it on the spot, you won't be at a loss for words. You can, if you want, combine your usual message with something personal, but it's best not to be at a loss for words when the time comes to sign a book.

MAKE A LIST OF YOUR KEY BUSINESS CONTACTS.

I suggest reading my book about business networking, *Business Dating*. I developed a system for myself, and eventually, my business coaching clients, to keep track of contacts and to know which type of contacts needed to be developed. It's called the 12x12™, and it will take the mystery out of who you need to know and develop relationships with in business, and you'll be able to use your book to begin or deepen each relationship.

In order from left to right (from "most likely" to "least likely" to refer you business), customize your columns and add people you know.

Authors					
1.					
2.					
3.					
4.					
5.					
6.					
7.					
8.					
9.					
10.					
11.					
12.					

Possible Categories: Authors, Entrepreneurs, Investors, Business Owners, etc. Chose the best options for your book and business growth.

SECOND, MAKE A LIST OF KEY PEOPLE YOU KNOW WHO AREN'T ON YOUR 12x12™.

The 12x12™ only covers the 144 most important people you need to know in business. And I'm sure you know lots of other people who can benefit from reading your book. Make a second list and be sure to get your book in their hands, too.

_____ _____

_____ _____

_____ _____

_____ _____

_____ _____

_____ _____

_____ _____

_____ _____

_____ _____

_____ _____

_____ _____

Do Seven Marketing Actions Every Day.

Identify the seven most important actions you can take, consistently, day in and day out, to market your business with your book (such as, give out five books a day, follow-up with one person I sent the book to, do a podcast interview about my book, etc.)

1. _____

2. _____

3. _____

4. _____

5. _____

6. _____

7. _____

Master List of Book Marketing & Client-Finding Strategies

1. _____

2. _____

3. _____

4. _____

5. _____

6. _____

7. _____

8. _____

9. _____

10. _____

11. _____

12. _____

13. _____

14. _____

15. _____

16. _____

17. _____

18. _____

19. _____

20. _____

21. _____

22. _____

23. _____

24. _____

25. _____

Let's Get Ninja

You don't need to spend thousands of dollars marketing your book. Following are low-cost and highly-effective strategies to get your book in the hands of the people who ultimately would benefit from hiring you.

Give books away.

Yup, I've said this before. Because I want you to do it! (For real.)

Strategic partner gifts.

Some of your best referral sources won't ever write a book, which means they can generate more business for themselves and you by passing out your book. Make a list of your strategic partners who might want to buy multiple copies of your book to give away:

_____

_____

_____

_____

_____

_____

Custom Printed Books.

Some of your strategic partners might even want to put their contact information (in lieu of the book description and your bio) on the back of your book (instead of placing their business card inside). Make a list of your strategic partners who might want to do a custom printing of your book to give away:

_____

_____

_____

_____

_____

_____

_____

_____

_____

_____

_____

_____

_____

_____

_____

_____

_____

_____

Use Postcards.

Have postcards printed with your book cover on one side, and a simple message pre-printed on the other side (such as: *I would love to send you a free copy of my book!*). Have ten postcards strategically mailed out every day to prospective readers or even professionals who might want to buy multiple copies of your book or do a custom printing.

Bookmarks are awesome, too.

Bookmarks are another option, and they are easier to carry around in quantity. If you're hosting a booth at a trade show or attending a conference with hundreds of people, bookmarks can be an easy way to share your book. You can get creative with the text you put on the bookmark, such as using a QR code that directs them to your BookFunnel link (where they can download the ebook for free), or to your two-chapter sample.

Stamps.

I get stamps made of each of my books, and they come in handy because I write several thank you notes every day. They are great conversation starters, and you never know who is going to catch a glimpse of your book in the form of a stamp and become a reader. I get my stamps through USPS.com.

Seeding the Market.

I love to leave my books, bookmarks, and postcards everywhere I go. Here are just a few of the places I leave them:

- Doctors' offices.
- Starbucks Coffee Shops.
- Airports and airplanes (such as in the backseat pockets of airplanes).
- Bookstores (inside of similar books).
- Hotel rooms.
- Taxis, subways, buses, and shuttles.

Make a list of places you can leave your book:

_____

_____

_____

_____

_____

_____

_____

_____

Your family and friends are part of your marketing team.

Your friends and family know people, and they travel, too. Because they like nice birthday and holiday gifts, I'm sure they won't mind if you ask them to help you get the word out about your book. Load them up with a few copies of your book, as well as any other collateral material you produce.

Make a list of your friends and family who will want to help you sell your books:

_____

_____

_____

_____

_____

_____

_____

_____

_____

_____

_____

_____

_____

_____

_____

_____

_____

_____

_____

_____

ASK READERS TO CHANGE THEIR FACEBOOK PHOTO TO THE COVER IMAGE OF YOUR BOOK. BE SURE TO PROVIDE THEM WITH THE SQUARE VERSION OF YOUR BOOK COVER [WHICH YOU'LL ALSO USE FOR THE AUDIOBOOK VERSION].

☙

# of Books	Places You've Left Them

# of Books	Places You've Left Them

THINK LIKE A NINJA

Brainstorm ten new ideas every day for marketing ideas for your book.

MONDAY	TUESDAY

WEDNESDAY	THURSDAY

FRIDAY	SATURDAY

143

End of Book Stuff

As with *Prosperity for Writers*, several readers requested a special place to do the exercises I suggested. This Workbook was the inspiration of a few people from my advanced reader team who felt like they needed a place to capture their book idea, and at the same time craft their book.

Two years ago, I did a series of videos with the awesome folks at Amazon's Kindle Direct Publishing for a promotion they did in January 2017 called "New Year, New Stories." You can watch them here: https://www.facebook.com/KindleDirectPublishing/. This promotion was designed to encourage new and aspiring authors to set New Year's writing resolutions. It was surreal to be surrounded by the Amazon staff, and hopefully helping and encouraging indie authors to write their books. It was such an incredible experience. Amazon loves their indie authors, as evidenced by my trip to Seattle. I encourage you to set your New Year's Resolutions this year, and every year, even if you're not being videotaped (or no one will know).

I didn't talk about the "book babies" that are the result of people reading this Workbook and the original *You Must Write a Book*. When I was interviewed by an Amazonian (who shall remain nameless, but of whom I am very fond) about how I would judge the success of *You Must Write a Book*, I said I would know it was successful by the number of "book babies" it inspired. I'm hoping for something like the great New York City blackout of 1977. So, if you've read either of these books and you write your book, I want to know about it. And I will definitely buy it! Just send me an email to Honoree@HonoreeCorder.com and let me know.

Happy writing, and thanks for reading! I can't wait to read *your* book!

Resources

Access to *I Must Write My Book* Bonuses

Go to HonoreeCorder.com/IMustBonuses for:

Action Plan Example & Template

Publishing Checklist

Podcast Request Email Template

Interview Sheet

Two-chapter Opt-In Sequence Example

12x12 Template

Book Giveaway Spreadsheet

Daily Brainstrom Spreadsheet

Blogs

The 5 Components of a Bestseller
http://honoreecorder.com/the-5-components-of-a-bestseller/

Advertising for Authors
http://selfpublishingformula.com/facebook-advertising-for-authors/

New Year, New Stories
http://honoreecorder.com/new-year-new-stories/

Best Book Business Reads

The Power of Consistency: Prosperity Mindset Training for Sales and Business Professionals (Weldon Long)

http://tinyurl.com/PowerofConsistency

On Writing: A Memoir of the Craft (Stephen King)

http://tinyurl.com/SKingOnWriting

Your First 1000 Copies: The Step-by-Step Guide to Marketing Your Book (Tim Grahl)

http://tinyurl.com/First1000Copies

You Must Write a Book: Boost Your Brand, Get More Business, and Become the Go-To Expert (Honorée Corder)

http://tinyurl.com/YouMustWriteaBook

The Miracle Morning for Writers: How to Build a Writing Ritual That Increases Your Impact and Your Income (Hal Elrod & Steve Scott, with Honorée Corder)

http://tinyurl.com/MM4Writers

Prosperity for Writers: A Writer's Guide to Creating Abundance (Honorée Corder)

http://tinyurl.com/ProsperityforWriters

The Nifty 15: Write Your Book in Just 15 Minutes a Day! (Honorée Corder & Brian Meeks)

http://tinyurl.com/Nifty15

The Prosperous Writer's Guide to Making More Money: Habits, Tactics, & Strategies for Making a Living as a Writer (Honorée Corder & Brian Meeks)

http://tinyurl.com/ProsperousWritersGuide

Like a Boss book series (Honorée Corder and Ben Hale)

http://tinyurl.com/LikeaBoss-BookSeries

Writing and Self-Publishing Podcasts

Authors' note: There are so many great podcasts, this is not the full list, just a few of my favorites to get you started:

The Author Biz Podcast
theauthorbiz.com

The Author Hangout
bookmarketingtools.com/blog

The Self-Publishing Podcast
sterlingandstone.net/podcasts

The Sell More Books Show
sellmorebooksshow.com/

The Smarty Pants Book Marketing Podcast
smartypantsbookmarketing.libsyn.com/podcast

The Wordslinger Podcast
kevintumlinson.com/podcast-rss

The Writer Files Podcast
rainmaker.fm

Quick Favor

I'm wondering, did you enjoy this book?

First of all, thank you for reading my book! May I ask a quick favor?

Will you take a moment to leave an honest review for this book on Amazon? Reviews are the BEST way to help others purchase the book.

Please leave your review where you bought this book
(and/or on Amazon and Goodreads).

SPECIAL INVITATION

Many like-minded individuals have gathered in an online community to share ideas, render support, and promote accountability. When I first wrote Prosperity for Writers, I envisioned helping numerous writers shatter the belief that they must starve to survive. I had no idea what was in store, and the result is an amazing community of thousands of writers, authors, editors, and more!

I'd like to personally invite you to join the Prosperous Writer Mastermind at HonoreeCorder.com/Writers and Facebook.com/groups/ProsperityforWriters where you will find motivation, daily support, and help with any writing or self-publishing questions.

You can connect with me personally on Twitter @Honoree, Linkedin.com/in/Honoree, or on Facebook.com/Honoree. Thank you so much for your most precious resource, your time. I look forward to connecting and hearing about your book soon!

GRATITUDE

I give thanks for my husband and daughter, without whom I wouldn't laugh nearly as much or be living the coolest life ever.

My team is incredible: Alyssa, Dino, Adam … you all make me look so good! Thank you!

Finally, I give thanks for everyone who has ever read one of my books and said something nice about it. This book is for you. I hope your book brings you as much joy and as many blessings as my books have brought to me.

Who is Honorée Corder

Honorée Corder is the author of dozens of books, including: *You Must Write a Book*; *I Must Write My Book*; *The Nifty 15: Write Your Book in Just 15 Minutes a Day!*; *The Prosperous Writers book series*; *Vision to Reality: How Short Term Massive Action Equals Long Term Maximum Results*; *Business Dating: Applying Relationship Rules in Business for Ultimate Success*; *The Successful Single Mom book series*; *If Divorce is a Game, These are the Rules*; *and The Divorced Phoenix.*

She is also Hal Elrod's business partner in *The Miracle Morning* book series, and together they've published fourteen titles to date. Honorée coaches business professionals, writers, and aspiring non-fiction authors who want to publish their books to bestseller status, create a platform, and develop multiple streams of income. She also does all sorts of other magical things, and her badassery is legendary. You can find out more at HonoreeCorder.com.

Honorée Enterprises, Inc.
Honoree@HonoreeCorder.com
http://www.HonoreeCorder.com
Twitter & Instagram: @Honoree

Facebook: http://www.facebook.com/Honoree

BOOK HONORÉE TO SPEAK

Honorée —you got me fired up! Thank you for building my confidence! Honorée's presentation was the perfect kick-off and her message of visualizing success was spot-on.
~Johnny B Truant, COO Sterling Stone

Honorée really captured the attention of our tribe, which is no easy task. Her quick-witted take on the world had them riveted—and keep in mind she followed Brooke Shields. Her stories are real, completely relatable, and just the sort of motivation women need to bring out their best.
~India Hicks, Founder, India Hicks Inc.

If you want engaging, results-oriented content without any fluff, I highly recommend booking Honorée Corder to speak at your event.
~Hal Elrod, Best-selling Author,
The Miracle Morning

Honorée Corder is THE self-publishing expert, but that's not all. For almost 20 years she's inspired and guided professionals to double their income and triple their time off. Her genuine charm and expert knowledge are guaranteed to help your audience, business, or group achieve the success they desire, all while laughing along the way.

Book Honorée as your Keynote Speaker and you're guaranteed to make your event highly energizing and valuable!

For more information visit **www.HonoreeCorder.com/speaking**

www.ingramcontent.com/pod-product-compliance
Lightning Source LLC
Chambersburg PA
CBHW080315220326
41519CB00071B/7126